RHODE ISLAND

in words and pictures

BY DENNIS B. FRADIN

ILLUSTRATIONS BY RICHARD WAHL

MAPS BY LEN W. MEENTS

Consultant

Laura B. Roberts
Curator for Education
Rhode Island Historical Society

CHILDRENS PRESS ®

CHICAGO

For my editor, Mary Reidy

For their help, the author thanks the staff members of the Rhode Island Historical Society. For help in obtaining photographs, the author thanks Edward Metcalf, Jr., Rhode Island Department of Economic Development.

Autumn in Rhode Island

Picture Acknowledgments:

COVER—Newport Harbor

RHODE ISLAND DEPARTMENT OF ECONOMIC DEVELOPMENT—
Cover, 2, 7, 9, 13, 14, 17, 19, 22, 23, 25, 26, 27, 29, 30, 33, 34, 35, 36, 37, 39, 41

RHODE ISLAND HISTORICAL SOCIETY—16

8 9 10 R 89

Library of Congress Cataloging in Publication Data

Fradin, Dennis B
  Rhode Island in words and pictures.

  SUMMARY: Brief introduction to the history of the smallest state and its geography, industries, cities, major tourist attractions, and famous citizens.
  1. Rhode Island—Juvenile literature.
[1. Rhode Island]   I. Wahl, Richard, 1939-
II. Meents, Len W.   III. Title.
F79.3.F73   974.5   80-22497
ISBN 0-516-03939-3

Rhode Island

Rhode (ROAD) Island is a state in the northeastern United States. Islands make up part of its land area. But most of the state is not an island.

Rhode Island is the smallest state. When people compare sizes, they often mention Rhode Island. You'll read that Alaska, our biggest state, is 486 times as big as Rhode Island. You'll read that Texas is 220 times as big. Rhode Island proves, though, that a state doesn't have to be big to be great!

Rhode Island was founded by people who wanted religious freedom. It was one of the first colonies to grant people freedom of religion and speech. It was the *first* colony to declare itself free of England.

Do you know where Revolutionary War hero Nathanael Greene was born? Or where Gilbert Stuart—the artist who painted portraits of George Washington—was born? Do you know where the first national tennis championship was held? Or the first U.S. Open golf championship?

You'll see that the answer to all these questions is: Rhode Island!

Over a million years ago, the Ice Age began. Rhode Island was covered by ice sheets known as *glaciers*. At

times the ice was a mile thick. Glaciers smoothed the land. In places they carved valleys in the ground. Melting glaciers filled these valleys with water and turned them into lakes.

The first people arrived in Rhode Island at least 8,000 years ago. Stone tools of ancient people have been found in the state. The early people hunted deer. They also gathered clams and other shellfish along the coast of Narragansett (nair • ah • GAN • sit) Bay.

In more recent times, a number of Indian tribes lived in Rhode Island. The Narragansetts and Wampanoags (WAM • peh • no • ags) were the largest Indian tribes in Rhode Island. The Pequots (PEE • qwats) and the Niantics (ny • ANN • tiks) were also there. All these tribes belonged to a large group of Indians known as the Algonquian family.

The Indians hunted deer, bears, and birds. They fished with nets and spears. They grew corn, beans, and pumpkins.

The Indians lived in houses made of wooden poles, bark, and animal skins. They made canoes out of tree trunks. Beads, called *wampum,* were used as money.

The Indians loved music and dancing. They enjoyed sports. They used bones and sticks for playing a dice game. They played a kind of football game on Rhode Island beaches.

Above: Dutch Island Harbor light
Left: The "Viking" mill

No one knows for sure who first explored Rhode Island. Some say that Norsemen (men from Norway) arrived in about the year 1000. There is a stone tower in Newport. It may have been built by the Norsemen.

Miguel de Cortereal (me • GEL DA kor • tee • ree • AL) of Portugal is thought to have sailed along the coast in 1511. Giovanni da Verrazano (jo • VAN • ne DA vair • reh • ZAN • oh), an Italian who sailed for France, explored the region in 1524. Some people think it was Verrazano who gave Rhode Island its name. They say that he first gave the name to an island that reminded him of the Island of Rhodes (ROADS) in the Mediterranean Sea. Others think that the Dutch sailor Adriaen Block gave the area its name when he arrived in 1614.

The first non-Indian settler in Rhode Island was an Englishman named William Blackstone. Blackstone left England in the 1620s. He crossed the ocean, and settled in Massachusetts. Massachusetts got too crowded for him. In 1635 he went to Rhode Island. He built a house near what is now Lonsdale. Blackstone planted some apple trees. He spent much of his time reading books.

William Blackstone is remembered as the first non-Indian to settle in Rhode Island. But a man named Roger Williams was the one who started a colony there. Roger Williams was born in London, England, in about 1603. He became a minister. In the 1600s people in England could not follow the religion they chose. Roger Williams knew that was wrong. He left England. He went to Massachusetts. But Roger Williams found that Massachusetts people didn't allow freedom of worship either. People who weren't Puritans were treated badly.

Roger Williams spoke out. He said that all people should be allowed to follow whatever religion they wanted. This sounds fair today. But Massachusetts

A statue of Roger Williams stands in Roger Williams Park in Providence.

people didn't agree with Roger Williams. Williams angered people for another reason. He said that the land in America really belonged to the Indians. He said that settlers should buy land from the Indians rather than have it granted to them by the king of England.

Finally, Roger Williams was forced to leave Massachusetts. He lived for a while with the Indians in Rhode Island. In 1636 Roger Williams bought some land from the Indians. He and his followers founded a settlement. Williams named the settlement *Providence*. He felt that God had provided this place. Providence was the first non-Indian town in Rhode Island.

Roger Williams planned Providence as a place where people would have freedom of religion and speech. Some people liked the idea. More arrived. Roger Williams' wife and children came there. In several years there were over 100 people in Providence.

Other people in search of religious freedom came to Rhode Island. Anne Hutchinson, William Coddington, and John Clarke were three of them. In 1638 the three helped found the settlement that became known as Portsmouth. Coddington and Clarke then built the town of Newport in 1639. Another town, Warwick, was founded in 1643.

Roger Williams felt that the four towns in Rhode Island should be united. This happened in 1647. From 1654 to 1657 Williams was the president of the Rhode Island colony.

Most people were farmers. They chopped down trees to clear fields. They built wooden houses. Then they grew corn and squash. The people kept cows for milk. Chickens provided eggs and meat. Sheep gave them meat and wool. The settlers also fished and hunted.

Do you remember William Blackstone, the first Rhode Island settler? He and Roger Williams became friends. Blackstone rode around Providence on a bull. He gave the children apples from his trees.

Because of their friendship with Roger Williams, the Indians were helpful. When food was scarce, they sometimes brought corn and turkeys to the settlers.

As more settlers arrived in the area, some Indians grew angry. They were losing their lands. Once, the Pequot and Narragansett Indians were talking about war. Roger Williams got into a canoe. He went to their meeting in Wickford. That time he talked them out of fighting.

A portrait of
King Philip
painted by Charles Brownell

War with the Indians did come in 1675. An Indian
called King Philip felt that his people would soon lose all
their lands. He led attacks against the settlers
throughout the big area known as *New England*.
Hundreds of settlers were killed. Towns were burned.

British sailors watch an Indian ceremonial dance in Charlestown.

The settlers formed an army. In 1675 the Indians were beaten in the "Great Swamp Fight" near Kingston. The next year King Philip was killed. King Philip's War, as it is called, ended in 1678. King Philip was proven correct. Many Indians were driven out. Today only about 1,500 Indians live in the whole state.

By 1708 over 7,000 settlers lived in Rhode Island. People began to do other things besides farm. Rhode Island lies near the Atlantic Ocean. People went out on ships to hunt for whales. The whale oil was used in oil lamps. Shipbuilding also became important. Candles, guns, and metal products were made in Rhode Island towns. Products were traded in colonies in America.

From 1754 to 1763 England and France fought a war in America. This is called the French and Indian War. To pay for this war, England placed heavy taxes on the American colonists.

People in Rhode Island—and in other American colonies—didn't want to pay these taxes. Besides, many didn't think of themselves as English any more. They had built towns and farms in America. They thought of themselves as Americans. "Let's make our own country," people said. They knew that they might have to fight a war with England to form it.

Burning the *Gaspee*, painted by Charles Brownell

One of the first acts leading to war occurred in Rhode Island. In 1769 Rhode Island people burned the English ship *Liberty* in Newport Harbor. In 1772 Rhode Islanders burned another English ship, the *Gaspee*. In 1776 Rhode Island became the first colony to declare itself free of England.

The war to free the American colonies from England is called the Revolutionary War. There was only one big battle in Rhode Island. England held Newport. The colonists tried to capture Newport in August 1778. They lost. That was called the Battle of Rhode Island.

Above: Redwood Library in Newport was built in 1748. It
was used by the British as an officers club during the
Revolutionary War.
Right: A memorial to the first black regiment to fight for
the American flag, in the Battle of Rhode Island.

Rhode Island sent about 6,000 men to fight on the American side. One Rhode Island man, Esek Hopkins, became the first commander of the American Navy. Nathanael Greene, who had been born in Warwick, became a great American general. He led soldiers to big wins in the South.

By 1783 the Americans had won the Revolutionary War. A new country—the United States of America—had been born!

Rhode Island became the 13th state on May 29, 1790. During its first 110 years of statehood, each county in Rhode Island had a capital. It wasn't until 1900 that Providence became the state's one and only, permanent capital. Over the years, Rhode Island was given several nicknames. It was called the *Ocean State* because of the importance of the Atlantic Ocean. It was called *Little Rhody* because of its small size. You might enjoy one fact about our smallest state. It has the longest official name! Its full name is *State of Rhode Island and Providence Plantations*.

Manufacturing (making things in factories) became important to Rhode Island in the late 1700s and early 1800s. Cloth making became very important. In England, cloth was made by machines. But before 1790, work was still done by hand in the United States. England kept

Above: Fort Adams was built in 1799 to defend the east passage of Narragansett Bay.
Left: Whitehall, built in 1729, is called the "Seat of American Culture."

their machines secret. It was against the law for English people to tell anyone how the machines were made. Cloth makers couldn't even leave England.

A young man named Samuel Slater worked in an English cotton factory. He saw how the machines worked. He memorized everything about them. Slater left England on a ship. According to a story, he did it by pretending to be a farm boy. In 1790 Slater set up the first power machines in the United States for making cotton yarn. This was at Pawtucket. Samuel Slater helped develop the textile (cloth making) industry in Rhode Island and the whole United States.

Another Rhode Island man, Nehemiah (nee • ah • MY • ah) Dodge of Providence, helped start our country's jewelry business. Silverware, paint, guns, and sewing machines were other Rhode Island products of the 1800s.

Many people who worked in Rhode Island's factories could not vote. Only rich landowners had that right. Thomas Dorr, a state lawmaker, wanted more people to be allowed to vote. In 1842, Dorr tried to take over the state government. This famous event in Rhode Island history is called "Dorr's Rebellion."

Dorr was stopped from taking over the government. He was put in prison. But thanks partly to him, Rhode Island adopted a new state constitution in 1843. These laws allowed more people to vote. This state constitution is the one that is still in effect.

In the 1860s, a much bigger fight than Dorr's Rebellion shook the United States. People in the North and the South had argued for years about slavery. They had argued over taxes and other issues. Fighting began in 1861. This was the start of the Civil War.

Rhode Island was in the North. About 24,000 Rhode Island men fought on the Northern side. They helped the North win the Civil War.

Mohegan Bluff on Block Island

In the 1900s farming became less important in Rhode Island. Manufacturing became much bigger than farming. Factories that made chemicals and metal products were built. People from around the world came to work in those factories. During World War I (1914-1918) and World War II (1939-1945) Rhode Island shipyards built many ships.

Since Rhode Island lies near the ocean, it is sometimes hit by hurricanes. Hurricanes are huge storms that form over the ocean. They hit land with winds over 100 miles

Beavertail Lighthouse in Jamestown. The 1938 hurricane uncovered the base of a lighthouse built here earlier.

per hour. They cause floods that sweep away people, buildings, and cars. In 1938 a big hurricane struck Rhode Island. Eight feet of water covered Providence. Over 300 people were killed in the state. Some people in Rhode Island today can tell you about this hurricane.

Work was done to protect Rhode Island. A dam was built on the Providence River in 1966. It helps keep Providence from flooding if a hurricane hits. Today, satellites out in space take pictures of hurricanes. People are warned when one is coming.

Today, Rhode Island is an important manufacturing state. It is a leader in making jewelry and textiles. About nine out of ten of the state's people live in cities. Only about one person in ten lives in a farm area.

You have learned about some of Rhode Island's history. Now it is time for a trip—in words and pictures—through the Ocean State.

Rhode Island is only 37 miles across in its widest distance from east to west. It is only 48 miles in its greatest distance from north to south. Yet this small state has many kinds of scenery. Rhode Island has forests, lakes, and hills. It has a lovely ocean coast. It has many rivers. It has big cities, farms, and islands.

Top right: Narragansett Beach
Above: Wickford Harbor
Left: Fall colors

Pretend you're in an airplane high above Rhode Island.
To the east and south you can see Narragansett Bay,
Rhode Island Sound, and Block Island Sound. These
bodies of water lead into the Atlantic Ocean. Providence
and most of the state's other big cities lie near
Narragansett Bay.

Providence

Your airplane is landing. You have arrived in
Providence. Providence is the biggest city in Rhode
Island. It is also the capital of the state.

Visit the Roger Williams National Memorial in
Providence. There you can learn about the "Father of
Rhode Island." Not far away visit the First Baptist

Above: Roger Williams Park in Providence
Left: Benefit Street, Providence

Church in America. A sign outside the church tells you that it was founded by Roger Williams in 1638.

The hilly streets of Providence have many houses from the 1700s. Visit the Governor Stephen Hopkins House, which was built in about 1707. Stephen Hopkins was governor of Rhode Island ten times. He also signed the Declaration of Independence. On Meeting Street visit the Brick School House, built in 1768. It was one of the first public schools in Providence. Today, the Providence Preservation Society is located there. This group works to keep Providence's old buildings looking like they did 200 years ago.

Providence has some great, modern schools. Brown University is in the city. It is one of the oldest universities in the country. Providence College, Rhode Island College, and the Rhode Island School of Design are also in the city.

Visit the Museum of Art in Providence. There you can see paintings by Manet (ma • NAY) and other famous artists. The works of art from ancient Greece and Rome are interesting, too.

You'll also enjoy the Roger Williams Park Museum of Natural History. There you can learn about Indian people, wildlife, rocks, and Narragansett Bay. Would you like to learn about Rhode Island history? Then visit the Museum of Rhode Island History in Providence.

Lawmakers from all over the state meet in Providence, in the State Capitol building. This white building is one of the best-looking capitols in the country. If the state lawmakers are meeting, you can watch them.

Above: Rhode Island State Ballet Company
Left: The State Capitol building

In recent years they have worked to stop air and water pollution in the state. They have worked on laws to help older people. They have worked on bills to improve travel in their state.

Roger Williams would be happy to see the variety of people in Providence today. There are people of many religions. There are people of different races and ethnic groups.

Designing silver

The people of Providence work at many different jobs.
Some make jewelry. Providence is the leading jewelry
making city in the United States. Rings, gold chains, and
earrings are some of the jewelry made there. Machinery,
silverware, cloth, and metals are also made in
Providence. Products made in the city go by train, boat,
truck, and plane to other cities of the world.

After seeing Providence, visit Warwick to the south. Warwick was founded by English settlers in 1643. Today it is the second biggest city in the state.

Do you remember how Rhode Islanders burned the English ship *Gaspee* in 1772? You can see where this happened, at Gaspee Point, in Warwick.

The Warwick Museum is interesting, too. There you can learn about the history of Rhode Island's second biggest city.

Today, watches and jewelry are made in Warwick. Many metal products are made in the city.

If you enjoy watching airplanes take off and land, you'll love Warwick. The Theodore Francis Green State Airport is in the city. It is the largest airport in Rhode Island.

Cranston, another of Rhode Island's largest cities, lies between Providence and Warwick. Cranston was first settled in about 1638 by some friends of Roger Williams.

Visit the Governor Sprague (SPRAIG) Mansion in Cranston. Rhode Island had two governors named William Sprague. One was uncle to the other. Both were born and lived in this house.

Visit the city of Pawtucket, just a few miles northeast of Providence. It was founded in 1671. *Pawtucket* is an Indian word meaning *the place by the waterfall.*

It was in Pawtucket that Samuel Slater built the first power machines for making cotton yarn. A lot of clothes are made in Pawtucket today.

Visit the Slater Mill Historic Site in Pawtucket. There you can see how Samuel Slater used waterpower to run his machines. The Slater Mill is nicknamed the *Cradle of American Industry.* It helped bring on the machine age in American factories.

The Slater Mill Historic Site

The city of Woonsocket (woon • SOCK • et) is about 10 miles northwest of Pawtucket. *Woonsocket* is another Indian word. It means *at the very steep hill.* Textiles, sporting goods, and Christmas ornaments are just some of the products made in Woonsocket.

After seeing some of Rhode Island's cities, take a trip through the countryside. You'll still see farms in the state. Apples, peaches, and potatoes are grown by Rhode Island farmers. Some farmers raise milk cows. Others

Little Compton

raise turkeys and chickens. A very famous kind of
chicken was first raised in Rhode Island. It is called the
Rhode Island Red. At the town of Little Compton there
is a monument. It reminds people that Rhode Island Reds
originated in that town in 1854.

About two-thirds of Rhode Island is covered by
forests. You'll see birch, hickory, and oak trees in the
state. A lot of wild animals live in the woodland and lake
areas. You may see deer, foxes, minks, and raccoons.
Ducks, pheasants, and quail can be found. You may see
owls. Sea gulls and other sea birds live near the coast.

You won't see any mountains in Rhode Island. But you
will see hills in the western part of the state. Jerimoth
(JER • eh • muth) Hill, in the northwest, is the state's

Above: Fishing in fresh water
Left: A tuna caught in salt water

highest point. It is 812 feet above sea level. The state's lowest point is sea level, along the coast.

Head back east, then take a trip down the coast. You'll see fishing boats going out into the Atlantic Ocean. Fishermen catch flounder, tuna, cod, and sea bass. Lobsters and clams are also caught.

You'll see lighthouses along the coast. The lights help guide boats to shore. You'll also see people boating, swimming, and sunning themselves along the coast.

There are 36 islands off the mainland. They are part of the state, too. You can get to the islands by boat. You can also get to some of them on bridges.

Touro Synagogue

The biggest island is Aquidneck (ah • KWID • nek) Island. The city of Newport lies on this island.

Newport is one of the most interesting cities in the United States. It was founded in 1639 by some families from Massachusetts. It became home to many people who sought religious freedom. Quakers came there. Jewish people came, too. The oldest Jewish synagogue in the United States can be seen in Newport. It is called Touro Synagogue (TOUR • o SIN • ah • gog).

During the 1700s Newport was one of the leading shipping cities in the United States. Later many rich people came to live in Newport or to spend the summer there. Houses nearly as big as castles were built.

Some houses in Newport are like castles.
Top left: An aerial view of the Vanderbilt mansion
Bottom left: Marble House at night
Above: The Vanderbilt mansion called the Breakers

Go on a path called the "Cliff Walk" in Newport. There you can see many old mansions built near the seacoast. You'll enjoy the Marble House.

You'll enjoy the Old Colony House in Newport. When Newport was the capital of Rhode Island, this was where lawmakers met. In 1776 Rhode Island lawmakers stood on the balcony of this building. They told people gathered below that Rhode Island was free of England.

Newport has played a big part in United States sports history. The first United States tennis championship was held in Newport in 1881. In 1895 the first U.S. Open golf championship was held there.

Newport today is the scene of many boat races. The Newport-Bermuda Yacht (YOT) Race starts there. The famed America's Cup races are held there, too.

Places can't tell the whole story of Rhode Island. Many interesting people have lived in the state.

A famous Indian named Massasoit (mass • eh • SOYT) (1580?-1661) lived in Rhode Island. Massasoit was the chief of the Wampanoag tribe that lived in Rhode Island and Massachusetts. You probably have heard of the Pilgrims, who came to Massachusetts in 1620. Chief Massasoit made a peace treaty with the Pilgrims. He kept the peace his whole life. He and other Indians helped the Pilgrims survive in their new homes. King Philip, Massasoit's son, felt differently about the settlers. He led attacks against them during King Philip's War.

Gilbert Stuart (1755-1828) was born in North Kingstown, Rhode Island. He began to paint pictures

Gilbert Stuart's homestead in Saunder's Town

when he was 13 years old. Stuart learned to paint portraits—pictures of people. He is famous for his portraits of George Washington. One can be seen in the State Capitol building in Providence. You can visit the Gilbert Stuart Birthplace at North Kingstown.

Robert Gray (1755-1806) was born in Tiverton, Rhode Island. He became an explorer. Gray was the first person to sail around the world in a ship that flew the American flag. He was also the first American explorer to reach the Columbia River in the northwestern United States.

Oliver Hazard Perry (1785-1819) was another famous sailor from the Ocean State. Perry was born in South Kingstown. He became a United States Navy officer.

During the War of 1812, Perry led American ships to a big victory on Lake Erie. After the battle he said the famous words: "We have met the enemy, and they are ours." You can see a statue of Oliver Hazard Perry in Rhode Island. It is outside the State Capitol building.

Prudence Crandall (1803-1890) was born in Hopkinton, Rhode Island. She became a teacher. In 1833 she opened a school for black girls. This was at a time when black people were kept out of many schools. She is remembered as a great teacher who worked for the rights of black people.

George M. Cohan (1878-1942) was born in Providence. He came from a family of actors and singers. As a child, George M. Cohan performed with them. Later, he wrote popular plays and musicals. He starred in them himself. "I'm a Yankee Doodle Dandy," "You're a Grand Old Flag," and "Over There" are three great songs he wrote.

The Watch Hill lighthouse

Home to Chief Massasoit . . . Roger Williams . . .
Prudence Crandall . . . General Nathanael Greene . . .
and the Rhode Island Red chicken.

A state that has seacoast . . . farms . . . forests . . .
and big cities.

The first colony to declare itself free of England.

Today a leading jewelry and textile state.

This is the Ocean State — Rhode Island.

Facts About RHODE ISLAND

Area—1,214 square miles (the smallest state)

Greatest Distance North to South—48 miles

Greatest Distance East to West—37 miles

Borders—Massachusetts to the north and east; the Atlantic Ocean to the south; Connecticut to the west

Highest Point—812 feet above sea level (Jerimoth Hill)

Lowest Point—Sea level, on the Atlantic Coast

Hottest Recorded Temperature—104° (at Providence, on August 2, 1975)

Coldest Recorded Temperature—Minus 23° (at Kingston, on January 11, 1942)

Statehood—Our 13th state, on May 29, 1790

Origin of Name Rhode Island—Some think that Rhode Island was named by Giovanni da Verrazano for the island of Rhodes in the Mediterranean Sea. Others think that the name came from the phrase *Roodt Eylandt* (meaning *Red Island)* which the Dutch explorer Adriaen Block used to describe an island in Narragansett Bay

Capital—Providence

Counties—5

U.S. Senators—2

U.S. Representatives—2

State Senators—50

State Representatives—100

State Song—"Rhode Island," by T. Clarke Brown

State Motto—*Hope*

Nicknames—The Ocean State, Little Rhody

State Seal—Adopted in 1875

State Flag—Adopted in 1877

State Flower—Violet

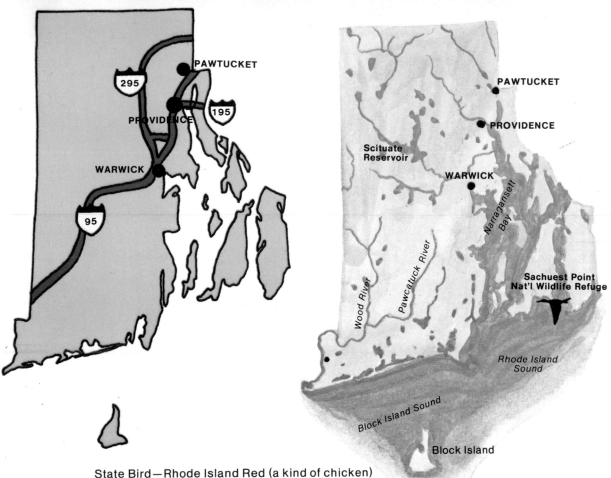

State Bird—Rhode Island Red (a kind of chicken)

State Tree—Red maple

Some Rivers—Blackstone, Moshassuck, Pawcatuck, Queens, Wood, Woonasquatucket, Pawtuxet, Providence

State Parks—20

Animals—Deer, foxes, rabbits, raccoons, minks, muskrats, many kinds of snakes, frogs, and turtles, pheasants, quail, ducks, owls, sea gulls, many other kinds of birds

Fishing—Flounder, clams, lobsters, tuna, sea bass, swordfish, cod, mackerel

Farm Products—Flowers, shrubs, trees, and other greenhouse and nursery products, milk, potatoes, apples, peaches, eggs, chickens, turkeys

Mining—Sand, gravel, granite, limestone

Manufacturing Products—Jewelry, silverware, metal products, textiles, boats, chemicals

Population—1980 census: 947,154 (1990 estimate: 995,501)

Major Cities	1980 Census	1990 Estimate
Providence	156,804	151,391
Warwick	87,123	no estimate
Cranston	71,992	no estimate
Pawtucket	71,204	70,512
East Providence	50,980	no estimate
Woonsocket	45,914	45,222

43

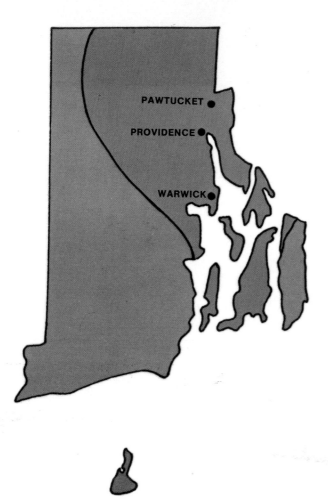

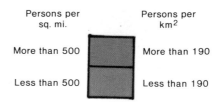

Persons per sq. mi.		Persons per km²
More than 500		More than 190
Less than 500		Less than 190

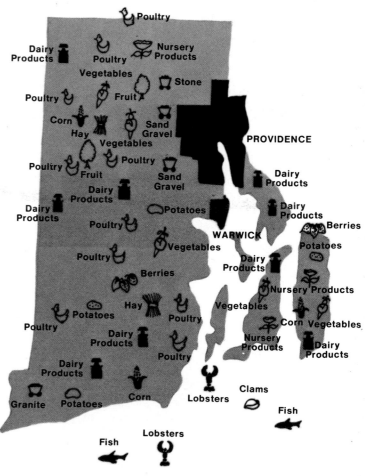

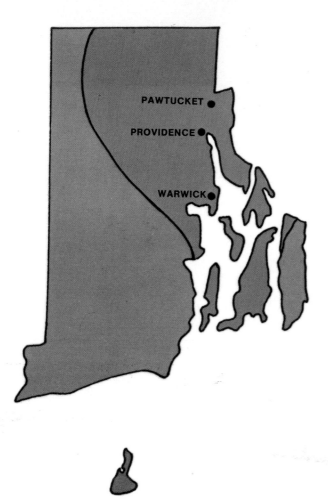

PAWTUCKET •

PROVIDENCE •

WARWICK •

Poultry

Dairy Products

Poultry

Nursery Products

Vegetables

Poultry

Fruit

Stone

Corn

Hay

Sand Gravel

Vegetables

Poultry

Fruit

Poultry

Sand Gravel

PROVIDENCE

Dairy Products

Dairy Products

Dairy Products

Potatoes

Berries

Poultry

WARWICK

Potatoes

Poultry

Vegetables

Dairy Products

Nursery Products

Berries

Corn Vegetables

Potatoes

Hay

Poultry

Vegetables

Poultry

Nursery Products

Dairy Products

Poultry

Dairy Products

Dairy Products

Lobsters

Clams

Granite

Potatoes

Corn

Lobsters

Fish

Fish

Lobsters

Rhode Island History

There were people in Rhode Island at least 8,000 years ago.

1511—The Portuguese sailor Miguel de Cortereal may have explored the Rhode Island coast in this year

1524—Giovanni da Verrazano, an Italian sailing for France, explores Narragansett Bay

1614—Dutch sailor Adriaen Block explores Block Island

1635—William Blackstone becomes the first non-Indian settler in Rhode Island

1636—Providence is founded by Roger Williams

1638—Anne Hutchinson, William Coddington, and John Clarke help begin the town of Portsmouth

1639—Newport is founded

1643—Warwick is founded by Samuel Gorton

1647—Providence, Portsmouth, Newport, and Warwick unite to form one Rhode Island colony

1675—In the first year of "King Philip's War," the Indians are beaten in the Great Swamp Fight near Kingston

1678—King Philip's War ends

1708—Population of colony is over 7,000

1723—Twenty-six pirates are hanged at Newport

1732—First Rhode Island newspaper, the *Rhode Island Gazette,* is published at Newport

1764—Brown University is founded

1769—Rhode Islanders burn the English ship *Liberty* in one of the first attacks against England in the colonies

1772—English ship *Gaspee* is burned by American patriots

1774—Rhode Island is the first colony to ban the bringing in of slaves

1775—Revolutionary War begins

1776—Rhode Island is the first colony to declare itself free of England

1783—Revolutionary War ends; about 6,000 Rhode Island men have helped the United States win it

1790—Rhode Island becomes our 13th state on May 29; in this same year Samuel Slater of Pawtucket builds the first power machines in the United States for making cotton yarn

1800—Population of Rhode Island is about 70,000

1815—Hurricane hits state

1842—Dorr's Rebellion results in a new state constitution allowing more people to vote

1854—Rhode Island Red chickens are first bred, at Little Compton

1861-1865—During the Civil War, Rhode Island sends supplies, soldiers, and the famous General Ambrose E. Burnside to help the North win

1892—University of Rhode Island is founded

1900—Providence becomes the state's one and only, permanent capital

1901—State Capitol building opens for use

1917-1918—During World War I, 28,817 Rhode
Islanders serve; ships for the war effort are built in the state

1938—Hurricane kills over 300 people in Rhode Island

1941-1945—During World War II, 92,027 Rhode Island men and women serve;
Rhode Island again builds ships for the war effort

1954—Rhode Island Red is made the state bird

1960—The first completely mechanized post office in the United States opens
at Providence

1966—Dam to protect Providence from hurricane-caused floods is completed

1969—Newport Bridge over Narragansett Bay is finished

1971—Rhode Island lawmakers approve a personal income tax

1976—During the U.S. Bicentennial celebration, the "Tall Ships" visit Newport

1978—Rhode Island landowners and state officials make an agreement to
return some land to the Narragansett Indians; the Indians claimed that
the land was taken illegally from them over 100 years before

1987—Republican governor Edward D. DiPrete begins second term

1989—The National Park Service closed Moonstone Beach in the hopes that three
pairs of an endangered species, the piping plover, will return and mate

INDEX

About the Author:

Dennis Fradin attended Northwestern University on a creative writing scholarship and was graduated in 1967. While still at Northwestern, he published his first stories in *Ingenue* magazine and also won a prize in *Seventeen's* short story competition. A prolific writer, Dennis Fradin has been regularly publishing stories in such diverse places as *The Saturday Evening Post, Scholastic, National Humane Review, Midwest,* and *The Teaching Paper*. He has also scripted several educational films. Since 1970 he has taught second grade reading in a Chicago school—a rewarding job, which, the author says, "provides a captive audience on whom I test my children's stories." Married and the father of three children, Dennis Fradin spends his free time with his family or playing a myriad of sports and games with his childhood chums.

About the Artists:

Len Meents studied painting and drawing at Southern Illinois University and after graduation in 1969 he moved to Chicago. Mr. Meents works full time as a painter and illustrator. He and his wife and child currently make their home in LaGrange, Illinois.

Richard Wahl, graduate of the Art Center College of Design in Los Angeles, has illustrated a number of magazine articles and booklets. He is a skilled artist and photographer who advocates realistic interpretations of his subjects. He lives with his wife and two sons in Libertyville, Illinois.

DATE DUE

#40089

974.5 FRA	Fradin, Dennis B Rhode Island in words and pictures

DATE DUE	BORROWER'S NAME	

40089

40089